CHARLES M. SCHULZ
creator of "Peanuts" says:

"On the wall of my studio I have an original Sunday page of B.C. given to me by Johnny Hart, and I often pause to admire it, for this page is a perfect work of comic strip art. The idea seems funnier every time I look at it, and the drawing is something for a student of comic art to study.

"Unfortunately, good drawing and fine pen technique have in these days become confused with slickness. Johnny Hart's B.C. has both good drawing, backed up with a fine pen technique, and consistently good ideas.

"I recommend it to you for fun and as a study in excellent comic strip art. I am pleased that it is now in book form, so that all of us can read and reread these many good strips."

by Johnny Hart

FAWCETT GOLD MEDAL • NEW YORK

To Irwin and Grace
who made this book possible

HEY! B.C.

Published by Fawcett Gold Medal Books, a unit of CBS Publications, the Consumer Publishing Division of CBS Inc., by arrangement with Funk & Wagnalls.

ISBN: 0-449-13670-1

Printed in the United States of America

31 30 29 28 27 26 25

WELL - SO MUCH FOR THE WHOLE WORLD.

SNIF!

NIP
NIP
NIP
NIP
NIP
NIP
NIP
NIP
NIP
NIP
NIP
THAT'S WHAT YOU CALL SURVIVAL OF THE HUNGRIEST.

BIRDS ARE FABULOUS CREATURES --THEY CAN FLY, WALK, EAT, RUN, SLEEP, DRINK, WARBLE,

-- IN FACT, THE ONLY THING THAT MAKES US SUPERIOR TO BIRDS IS THE FACT --

GOOD MORNING, IDIOT.

THAT BLOWS THAT THEORY.

THERE'S THAT WHITE STUFF AGAIN.

GREAT ZOT! IT'S ONLY WATER!

--IT'S AWFUL FAT FOR WATER.

WHY SHOULD I WASTE MY TIME ON FAT WATER?

WILEY ?

--THOR ?
---PETER ?

-CLUMBY CARP ?

PETER! --
-- I JUST SAW MY PICTURE IN THE WATER!

IT'S NOT A VERY GOOD LIKENESS OF YOU!

I'VE BEEN STUDYING THE SUN ALL DAY!

WHAT DID YOU LEARN?

ZAK

NEVER TO STUDY THE SUN ALL DAY!

I HAVE MADE A PROFOUND CONCLUSION IN REGARD TO THE SUN.

WHAT'S THAT?

IT ONLY APPEARS DURING THE DAY.

YOU'RE A GENIUS, PETER.

IT IS MY PROFOUND CONVICTION THAT THE WORLD IS ROUND, INSTEAD OF FLAT!

LIKE, WE'RE RIGHT HERE!

NOW! - WE SAIL ALL THE WAY AROUND TO HERE -

THEN, WE FALL OFF.

MAKES ME SICK! ---EVERYONE ELSE HAS NICE NORMAL NAMES---
--THEN FOR NO EARTHLY REASON AT ALL THEY TAG ME WITH A STUPID NAME LIKE--
...
CLUMSY....
--CARP!
THE REASON I'M SO CLUMSY IS THAT I HAVE NO DIGNITY!
FROM NOW ON, I SHALL REEK OF DIGNITY!
STARTING WITH HUMBLE DIGNITY.

GREAT ZOT!
CLUMSY CARP
IS DROWNING!

GNASH
WHY DID YOU GO AND DO THAT? I WAS OBSERVING THE NATURAL HABITAT OF THE MARINE WORLD!

OF COURSE! --HOW STUPID OF ME.

THE LAST FLICKER OF SUNSET DIED INTO NIGHT WITH THE FINAL LINGERING NOTE OF THE DOOKEY BIRD. THE FISH SETTLED GRACEFULLY INTO

--INTO

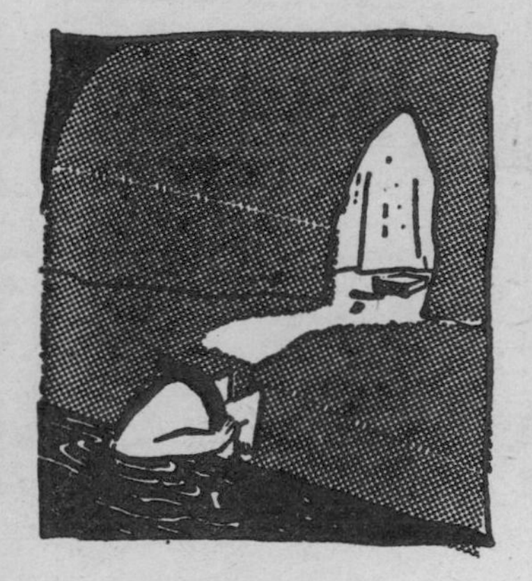

THE INKY DEPTHS -

HI, B.C.

WHAT ARE YOU MAKING NOW ?

LIGHTNING BOLTS!

YOU'D EXPECT SOMETHING LIKE THAT FROM A GUY NAMED THOR!

WHAT ARE YOU DOING NOW, THOR ?
I'M INVENTING A CALENDAR! -- A DEVICE WHICH TELLS YOU WHAT DAY IT IS.
WHAT DOES IT MATTER WHAT DAY IT IS ?
HOW ELSE WILL PEOPLE KNOW WHAT DAY I INVENTED THE CALENDAR?
WEDNESDAY THE ELEVENTH--
THURSDAY THE TWELFTH--
FRIDAY THE --
THIRTEENTH !

A ROLLING STONE GATHERS NO MOSS.

HOW COME YOU NEVER MAKE UP ANY POEMS ABOUT WATER, WILEY?
THE MERE MENTION OF THE WORD MAKES MY SKIN CRAWL!

MERCIFUL ZOT!
--I'M
TRAPPED!

AAARRRGGHH

GOT
ME!

WOE, THAT I SHOULD BE SO BLAND,

-ELSE I COULD YIELD A BLOTTER,

THAT SPREADETH OVER ALL THE LAND,

••AND SUCKETH UP THE WATER.

I THINK THAT I
SHALL NEVER SEE

A POEM LOVELY AS--

THE WORLD WILL HAVE TO
WAIT FOR JOYCE KILMER.

?

MY NAME IS CURLS.

WHAT DOES THAT MAKE ME ?

ONE OF THE UNFRIENDLIEST CRUMBS I'VE EVER MET!

I'D LIKE YOU TO MEET CURLS, MASTER OF SARCASTIC HUMOR.

LET'S HEAR YOU SAY SOMETHING FUNNY.

I'M PLEASED TO MEET YOU.

IT HAS COME TO MY REALIZATION THAT A PICTURE IS WORTH A THOUSAND WORDS.

CONGRATULATIONS!

YOU JUST IMPROVED YOUR VOCABULARY BY NINE HUNDRED AND EIGHTY-SEVEN WORDS.

WE'RE GOING TO HAVE A RACE, CURLS.

THE WHOLE THING IS MY IDEA. I THOUGHT IT UP!

I CALL IT 'THE HUMAN RACE!'

THAT DISQUALIFIES YOU.

I WITHDRAW, AN UTTER FAILURE.
B.C.

B.C.

WHAT'S THE TROUBLE, B.C. ?
IT'S THAT NEW PET OF MINE, PETER, --EVERYONE ASKS WHAT IT IS, AND I DON'T KNOW WHAT TO TELL THEM.

THAT'S EASY ENOUGH-- WHAT IS ITS MOST PREDOMINANT CHARACTERISTIC?
IT EATS ANTS!

WELL! ---THERE YOU ARE!
WHY, OF COURSE! ---IT'S AN EATANTER!

ZOT

WHAT FUNNY LOOKING ANTS.

THEY'RE RED!

CRUNCH

RAT-A-TAT
TAT-TAT
RAT-A-TAT
TAT-TAT-TAT
TAT-TAT
TAT-A-TAT

HI!
HELLO THERE.
WHAT WAS THAT ?

HERE COMES WILEY -- LOOKS LIKE HE'S SEEN A GHOST!

OVER THAT HILL! --- I JUST SAW SOME NEW TYPE OF CREATURE ---

GHASTLY, MENACING, SQUALID, INAUSPICIOUS, GROSS, CADAVEROUS!

HE LEFT OUT "STRIKING"!

PAT
PAT
PAT
PAT
PAT
PAT
PAT
PAT

A STRAIGHT LINE NEVER WAVERS.

AN ADDITIONAL STRAIGHT LINE PLACED THUSLY WILL GIVE US PARALLEL LINES.

PARALLEL LINES NEVER MEET.

WHO NEEDS THEM?

IT'S INEVITABLE THAT, IN TIME, WOMAN, THROUGH HER SUPERIOR INTELLIGENCE, WILL TRIUMPH OVER MAN.

THOSE NEW CREATURES SAY WOMAN IS GOING TO TRIUMPH OVER MAN.

HI! ---WE'RE EXPECTING A BIG BATTLE WITH WOMEN!
WHEN?

THAT'S HARD TO SAY --- WE DON'T EVEN KNOW WHAT THEY ARE YET!

SIMPLETONS

IN THE DARK HOUR OF HISTORY WHEN WOMAN THREATENS TO TRIUMPH OVER MAN, YOU SLEEP!

-- FOR ALL WE KNOW, WE MIGHT ALREADY BE TRIUMPHED OVER!

WOMAN HAS THREATENED TO TRIUMPH OVER US, CURLS, AND WE MAY AS WELL FACE IT! --NOT ONLY DON'T WE KNOW WHAT WOMAN IS--
--WE DON'T EVEN KNOW WHAT TRIUMPH MEANS!
NOW YOU KNOW THE MEANING OF TRIUMPH!

THOR FELL OUT OF A TREE TODAY!

THERE HE GOES NOW, POOR DEVIL.

WHAT'S THE BIT WITH THE HANDS?

HE TORE HIS SUIT OFF.

BEAR WITNESS, B.C., TO THE DISCOVERY OF GRASS!

TESTIFY THEE HENCE THE DISCOVERY OF FLOWERS!

WITNESS YE FURTHERMORE THE DISCOVERY OF---

--AN INCREDIBLE RESERVOIR OF STRENGTH!

BEAR WITNESS, B.C., TO THE DISCOVERY OF THE LEAF!

VERIFY THEE HENCE THE DISCOVERY OF SUCCULENT FRUITS!

WITNESS YE FURTHERMORE THE DISCOVERY OF SAND!

WHY COULDN'T I HAVE BEEN BORN A DISCOVERER INSTEAD OF A WITNESS?

BEAR WITNESS, B.C., TO THE DISCOVERY OF TOADSTOOLS!

TESTIFY THEE HENCE, THE DISCOVERY OF THE MUD PUDDLE!

WITNESS YE FURTHERMORE THE DISCOVERY OF THE CLAM!

WITNESS THOU, MOREOVER, THE DISCOVERY OF A DISCOVERER!

BEAR WITNESS, B.C., TO THE DISCOVERY OF STONE!

TESTIFY THEE HENCE, --THE DISCOVERY OF SOIL!

WITNESS YE FURTHERMORE THE DISCOVERY OF WATER!

I THINK I'LL GO DISCOVER SOME SLEEP.

ZOT

B.C.

...MORTIFIER...
-FALSIFIER--TERRIFIER
--CRUCI---

FIER!

HOW DO YOU THINK OF THOSE SPUR-OF-THE MOMENT NAMES, WILEY?

YOU'LL NOTICE, B.C., -- I HAVE PRODUCED MY OWN FIER.
HOW?
IT'S A CINCH ! -- YOU SIMPLY RUB A COUPLE STICKS TOGETHER.

YOU HAVE THE NEATEST HAIR IN THE WORLD.
I THINK I'M GOING TO PASS OUT FROM DISGUST!

SHE SAID I HAD THE NEATEST HAIR IN THE WORLD.
SIGH
I GUESS THIS PUTS THE SKIDS ON MY LOVE-LIFE!

--YOU HAVE THE CRUMMIEST HAIR IN THE WORLD!
FICKLE!

MY MESSY HAIR HAS ME ON THE OUTS WITH THOSE NEW CREATURES.
AN EVIL OMEN!
FOR YOUR PENANCE A FISHBONE MUST BE ENSCONCED IN YOUR HAIR!
HE SHOULD HAVE ENSCONCED IT IN MY BIG MOUTH!

I'M GETTING SICK OF WEARING THIS STUPID FISHBONE!

!

GREAT ZOT!-- I'VE INVENTED THE COMB!

THINK I'LL TRY MY NEW COMB ON WILEY.
Z
Z
Z
NAW---
Z
--WHO EVER HEARD OF A WELL-GROOMED SLOB?
Z

LOOK, B.C.! -- I'VE INVENTED THE WHEEL! ----THE MOST IMPORTANT DISCOVERY THE WORLD HAS EVER KNOWN!
WILL IT WORK?
WHO CARES?
THAT'S WHAT'S SO WONDERFUL ABOUT THIS WORLD --- YOU DON'T HAVE TO WORK TO BE IMPORTANT!

YOU'LL HAVE TO ADMIT IT, WILEY -- I'VE REALLY HIT IT BIG THIS TIME. -- WHO ELSE WOULD THINK OF INVENTING THE WHEEL!
WHAT'S IT GOOD FOR?
WHAT'S IT GOOD FOR?
IT'S GREAT FOR ROLLING DOWN HILLS!

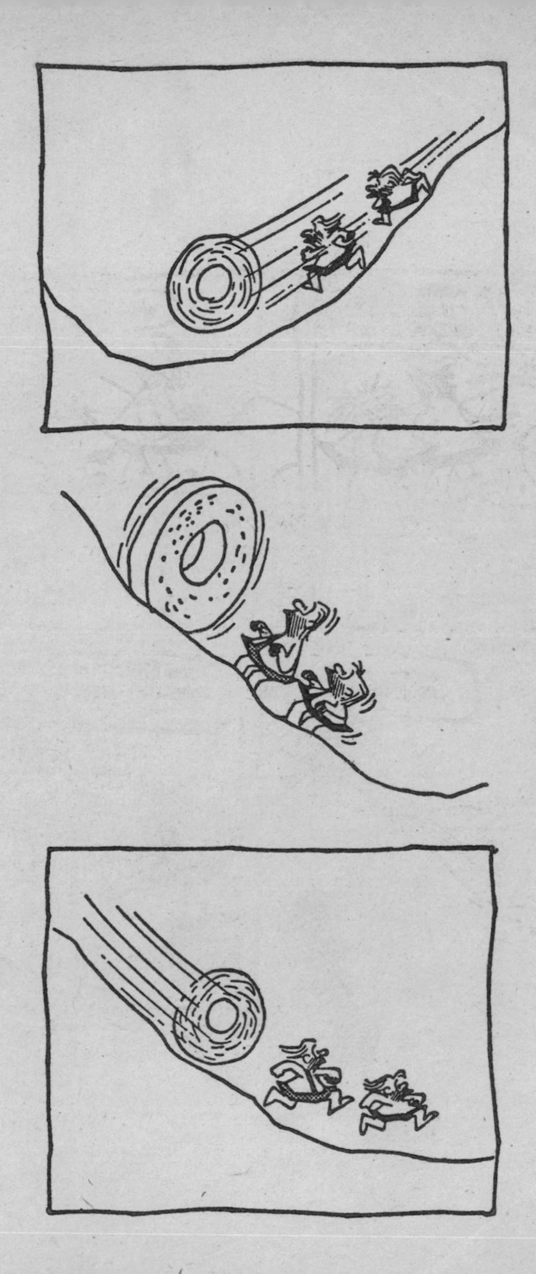

WHAT EVER INSPIRED YOU TO THINK OF THE WHEEL, THOR ?
I'LL NEVER TELL!
SOLD OUT BY MY OWN ACCOMPLICE!

I WAS WONDERING IF EITHER OF YOU-

HAS ANY ADVICE-

ON HOW TO INVENT BRAKES.

THERE.
JAMB
WHOP
I'VE INVENTED BRAKES!

I'M BEING FOLLOWED!

THEY KEEP FOLLOWING ME!

THERE'S NO ESCAPE!

I CAN'T GO ON!

GO AHEAD! STOMP ALL OVER ME!

I'M GETTING A FOOTPRINT COMPLEX.
I'M GETTING MENTALLY SICK!
US SICKIES HAVE TO STICK TOGETHER.

FOOTPRINTS, FOOTPRINTS, FOOTPRINTS, I THINK I'M GOING OUT OF MY MIND!

CUT THAT OUT!

THESE LITTLE INSIGNIFICANT FOOTPRINTS HAVE DRIVEN ME MAD!

IT MUST BE NICE TO HAVE YOUR OWN ERASER!

I'M OVERCOMING MY FOOTPRINT COMPLEX! THEY'RE ACTUALLY BEAUTIFUL!

SO SYMMETRICAL! SO MAJESTIC! SO COMPATIBLE!

NOW THERE GOES A MISERABLE MATCH!

WHAT ARE YOU MAKING, THOR ?

A PEDESTAL!

DON'T FORGET TO LEAVE ENOUGH SPACE BETWEEN THE TORUS AND THE PLINTH FOR A GOOD SIZED SCOTIA.

I GET THE STRANGE FEELING THAT THIS IS NOT A FIRST.

I HAVE INVENTED THE PEDESTAL.
WHAT'S IT FOR?
I FIGURE THE WOMEN CAN STAND AROUND ON IT!
IT WILL NEVER BE ACCEPTED BY SOCIETY.

I'LL GIVE YOU THREE CLAMS FOR YOUR PEDESTAL.
THREE CLAMS!! ARE YOU OFF YOUR NUT?

IN THE FIRST PLACE THE ECHINUS IS TOO WEAK TO SUPPORT THE ABACUS, AND WHAT'S MORE, YOU LEFT OUT THE ASTRAGAL ENTIRELY.

IF I FIND OUT YOU MADE UP THOSE WORDS YOU'RE GONNA GET BELTED RIGHT IN THE MOUTH!

UPON THIS SITE, I HEREBY ESTABLISH "THE PEDESTAL OF PROFOUND TRUTH."
TRUTH
AS I LOOK OUT AMONG YOU, I SEE THE FACES OF BRILLIANT MEN!
ZOT
NEVER LIE ON THE PEDESTAL OF TRUTH!
TRUTH

CIVILIZATION IS SOCIETY.
TRVTH

SOCIETY IS CIVILIZATION.

SOCIETY RULES CIVILIZATION, CIVILIZATION RULES SOCIETY—AND IN TIMES OF CRISIS, THEY RULE ONE ANOTHER!

SOMEDAY MEN LIKE PETER WILL RULE THE WORLD.
TRVTH

GO ON, B.C., SAY SOMETHING ON THE TRUTH PEDESTAL!
— I DON'T KNOW WHAT TO SAY!
AW, COME ON, B.C.
TRVTH

IT'S EASY! JUST BEIN ON THE PEDESTAL IS AN INSPIRATION!

TRVTH

DOWN WITH THE LIARS' CLUB!

HERE COMES WILEY, THE FABULOUS POET.

GOOD MORNING HIC
HOW LOVELY HIC

YOU'RE LOOKING HIC
THIS MORNING HIC

NOTICE HOW EVERYTHING RHYMED?

HERE COMES WILEY WITH THE HICCUPS.
HIC HIC

HIC
CLAP
HIC
CLAP
HIC

HIC
CLAP
HIC
SNAP
IS THERE NO PITY?

HIC
HIC
HIC

HIC
WHAM
HIC
WHAM
HIC
WHAM
HIC
WHAM

NEVER ENTER A CAVE WITH THE HICCUPS.
HIC HIC HIC

LET'S SCARE THE HICCUPS OUT OF WILEY!
WE'RE GOING TO THROW YOU IN THE CREEK, WILEY!

HOLD IT! .... HEY! -- THEY'RE GONE!!! THEY'RE GONE!

THANKS, FELLOWS!
WHEW!
HIC

THIS IS THE CLEVEREST TRAP YOU'VE THOUGHT OF YET, PETER!
SHUT UP AND KEEP DIGGING!
WHO ELSE WOULD THINK OF CAPTURING A DINOSAUR?
WE'RE GETTING DEEP
KEEP DIGGING
A DINOSAUR WON'T HAVE A CHANCE IF IT FALLS IN HERE!
IT SURE IS DARK DOWN HERE.
KEEP GOING!
HOW WILL WE GET THE POOR CRITTER OUT OF HERE?
?
?
HELP!

I KNOW HOW WE CAN ALL GET OUT OF THIS DINOSAUR PIT!
HOW?
WE JUST WAIT FOR RAIN! --THEN WHEN IT FILLS UP WITH WATER--
AAAAAARRRRGGGHHH
IT WAS JUST A THOUGHT, WILEY.

HEY! I'LL BET IF WE STOOD ON EACH OTHER'S SHOULDERS WE COULD GET OUT OF HERE!
GREAT IDEA!
ZOT
I HOPE YOU'RE SATISFIED! YOU CRUMMY LITTLE ANT-STABBER!

WE'VE TRIED EVERY POSSIBLE WAY WE CAN THINK OF TO GET ALL OF US OUT OF THIS PIT, CURLS -- WHAT SHALL WE DO NOW ?
YOU HAVEN'T TRIED THE SAME METHOD YOU USED TO GET IN !
WHAT'S THAT ?
MASS STUPIDITY!

WHAT AN IRONIC FATE! TRAPPED IN OUR OWN DINOSAUR PIT!
?

GREAT ZOT!

THE HUMILIATION IS UNBEARABLE!

MY FRIENDS AND I WOULD LIKE TO EXTEND OUR THANKS TO YOU FOR SAVING US FROM THAT PIT!

GRONK

STRONG WIND TODAY.

WHAT MAKES THE WIND BLOW, PETER ?

MORE OFTEN THAN NOT, IT IS A MOLECULAR REACTION, RESULTING FROM SUSTAINE EROSION, DIRECTLY INFLUENCE BY THE INTERNAL COMBUSTIO OF TREE ROOTS.

WHAT IS WIND ?

WIND IS A MASS OF AIR SET INTO VAGUE MOTION BY A QUESTIONABLE SOURCE.

THANK YOU.

YOU'RE WELCOME, WIND MOUTH!

I HAVE INVENTED THE WORLD'S FIRST WINDBAG!

WELL, WELL, I SEE YOU HAVE DEVISED A CRUDE BAG, WITH WHICH TO DETERMINE WIND DIRECTION!

NOT BAD! HOWEVER, I SEE YOU HAVE PROVIDED NO MEANS OF DETECTING VELOCITY, WHICH OF COURSE IS OF PRIMARY IMPORTANCE!

CORRECTION: YOU HAVE INVENTED THE WORLD'S SECOND WINDBAG!

I'M GOING TO TRY AN EXPERIMENT WITH THE NEW CREATURES.

IF THOR CAN GET KISSED
BY THOSE NEW CREATURES
I DONT SEE WHY I CAN'T.

UST TOSS THESE
N THAT CAVE, AND A
UTE LITTLE CREATURE
VILL KISS YOU.

WHACK

YOUR CONCEPTION OF 'CUTE,' AND MINE VARY CONSIDERABLY

I GOT KISSED BY ONE OF THOSE NEW CREATURES.
GREAT ZOT! THE CURSE OF THE WICKED--

--FOR YOUR PENANCE YOU ARE BANISHED TO A PITFUL OF ITCHY-LEAVES AND FORBIDDEN TO SPEAK----

--UNTIL THE MOON HAS RISEN FULLY IN THE EVENING SKY!

I DON'T DISCOURAGE THIS EASY!

PITCH BLACK NIGHTS
ARE KISSING NIGHTS!
WATCH THIS!

SMACKITY
SMACK
SMACK
SMACKITY
SMACK

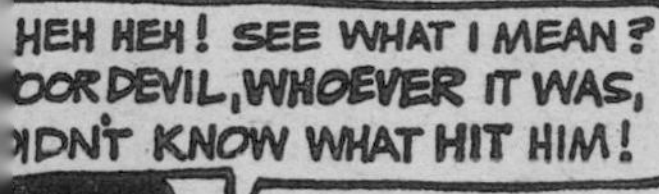
HEH HEH! SEE WHAT I MEAN?
OOR DEVIL, WHOEVER IT WAS,
IDN'T KNOW WHAT HIT HIM!

ZOT

I HAVE INVENTED THE COMPASS TO SUPPLEMENT YOUR NEW DIRECTIONAL SYSTEM.

IT ALWAYS POIN
NORTH!

WHY, THAT'S AMAZING! HOW DOES IT WORK?

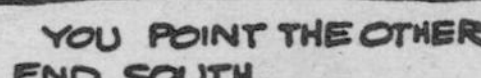

YOU POINT THE OTHER END SOUTH.

THE SUN ALWAYS RISES IN THE NORTH, AND A COMPASS ALWAYS POINTS TO THE NORTH.

KEEP YOUR EYE ON THAT HILL OVER THERE, THE SUN WILL BE RISING ANY MINUTE NOW.

HOW DO YOU LIKE THAT! THE MISERABLE THING'S BUSTED ALREADY!

HERE COMES THE EATANTER.
HE'S BEEN SPYING ON THE WOMEN!
HE'S DRAWING SOMETHING IN THE SAND---
WHY, IT'S A LEVER! THOSE WOMEN HAVE INVENTED THE LEVER!
GOOD WORK, BENEDICT!

THEY'RE DEVELOPING A USE FOR THEIR NEW LEVER!
LET ME SEE!
KRUNCH
NOW WE'LL NEVER KNOW WHAT IT WAS.

WHAT ARE THOSE
WOMEN DOING?

THEY'RE STILL TRYING
TO DEVELOP A USE FOR
THEIR NEW LEVER.

THIS IS ONE TIME
WE'VE BEAT THEM TO
THE PUNCH!

WHAT IS THE MOON?

THE MOON IS A HOLE IN THE SKY THROUGH WHICH DAYLIGHT PASSES!

HOW CAN A **HOLE** MOVE FREELY THROUGH THE SKY?

NO RESPONSIBILITIES!

WHAT IS THE MOON, THOR?
YOU SEE, WHAT THAT IS---

THAT'S ONE OF THOSE ---THE REASON IT'S ROUND---THAT IS-

I HAVEN'T GOT ALL NIGHT, THOR.

WELL, THE MOON DOES!

THINK I'LL ASK B.C. WHAT THE MOON IS--

WHAT'S THAT?

THAT'S AN ENORMOUS BLACK BAT!

THERE'S THE MOST RIDICULOUS ANSWE I'VE HEARD YET!

I HAVE ASKED VARIOUS INDIVIDUALS TO DESCRIBE THE MOON. NOW IT'S YOUR TURN, CURLS.

IT'S A PRETTY SILLY HOUR FOR DESCRIPTIONS, ISN'T IT ?

COME ON, CURLS, WHAT IS THE MOON ?

IT'S A CONVERSATION PIECE FOR VICTIMS OF INSOMNIA!

KRACK

--THERE'S A SOLID DRIVE THAT'S GOING DEEP INTO RIGHT FIELD---

THUWHACK

OUT!

I HAVE INVENTED A GAME CALLED BASEBALL, PETER ---

A GAME WHEREIN YOU STRIKE A COCONUT WITH A CLUB AND --
HOLD IT!

--HOW DO YOU EXPLAIN THE TERM BASEBALL?

YOU STRIK THE BASE O A TREE TO OBTAIN THE BALL!

CRAAACCKK

WE'VE INVENTED A GAME CALLED FOOTBALL
YOU TRY TO KNOCK DOWN WHOEVER HAS THE BALL, BEFORE HE --
HAS A CHANCE TO--
CRUNCH
I CAN SEE YOU'RE ANXIOUS TO GET STARTED.
'JUST KEEP YOUR FINGER RIGHT THERE; EVEN AFTER I KICK THE COCONUT.
ZAP
BLAT
GREATER LOYALTY HATH NO TEAMMATE!

WANT TO PLAY ON OUR FOOTBALL TEAM, WILEY ?

DON'T BE SILLY, I CAN'T RUN WITH A PEG-LEG!

HOW ABOUT WATER-BOY?

AAAAAARRGGH

MAYBE WE OUGHT TO ASK THE WOMEN TO PLAY FOOTBALL WITH US!
NAW! WHAT DO THEY KNOW ABOUT IT?

ALL THEY KNOW HOW TO DO IS SIT AROUND ALL DAY SEWING SKINS TOGETHER.

HERE, DOGGIE!

COME ON, BOY--

THERE'S A "SICK ONE" FOR YOU.

SHE CALLED ME A DOGGIE!
I'M SO HUMILIATED I COULD KILL MYSELF.
I WONDER HOW A DOG WOULD GO ABOUT COMMITTING SUICIDE?

SHE CALLED ME A DOGGIE!.

I'M SO HUMILIATED I COULD DIE.

WHY NOT ?

--ALL I HAVE TO DO IS PULL THE TRIGGER.

HERE, DOGGIE, DOGGIE, DOGGIE!

RUN FOR IT, YOU FOOL! SHE'S UPON YOU!

WHAT AN INGLORIOUS WAY TO SUCCUMB--

PARALYZED WITH DISGRACE!

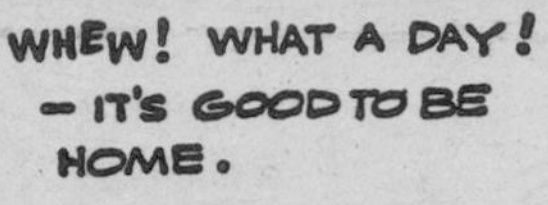
WHEW! WHAT A DAY! – IT'S GOOD TO BE HOME.

GET OUT OF HERE, YOU LITTLE PEST! GO FIND YOUR OWN CAVE!

GAD! CAN'T A GUY EVEN MAKE A MISTAKE?

WHEN THEY GO TO ALL THAT TROUBLE, YOU DON'T HAVE THE HEART TO EAT THEM!

THUMP
THUMP
THUMP
THUMP
THUMP
THUMP
THUM

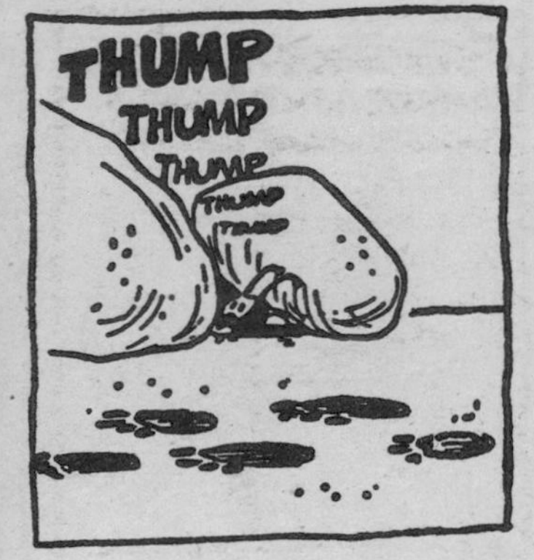
THUMP
THUMP
THUMP
THUMP

IT'S AN ANTEATER'S WORLD!

AAAAHHHH
ZOT
SOMEBODY UP THERE LIKES ME.

MY NEW INNOVATION–
THE SPHERICAL WHEEL!

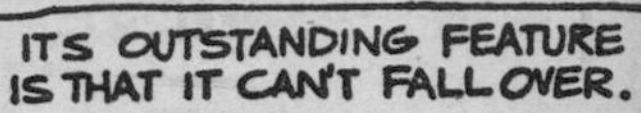
ITS OUTSTANDING FEATURE
IS THAT IT CAN'T FALL OVER.

EVER CONSIDERED
INVENTING THE BALL?

I'VE MADE AN IMPROVEMENT ON MY NEW WHEEL, B.C.

HOW DO YOU FIGURE THAT'S AN IMPROVEMENT?

IT CAN'T ROLL AWAY.

HI, B.C.

WHAT'S THAT, THOR ?
IT'S A HOOD.

WHAT HAVE YOU GOT IN THERE ?

NEXT YEAR'S WHEEL!

READY FOR THE UNVEILING! GENTLEMEN, BEHOLD!--

THE NEW WHEEL!

GEE!
BUT WHAT ARE THOSE THINGS?

GRIPPERS.

I HAVE MADE A REVOLUTIONARY NEW ADVANCE ON THE WHEEL!

SPOKES!
ANYTHING I COULD SAY NOW WOULD BE ANTICLIMACTIC!

IF ONLY I COULD THINK OF A PRACTICAL USE FOR THE WHEEL!

POOR THOR--DAY AFTER DAY HE SITS OUT THERE ON THAT ROCK.

SOMETHING SEEMS TO BE TROUBLING HIM. HE LOOKS SO SAD--

LET'S RIDE OUT AND SEE IF WE CAN COMFORT HIM.

THERE IS A LIMIT TO HOW MUCH A MAN CAN TAKE!

WOMEN INVENTED THE WHEEL FIRST! --THEY BEAT US TO THE PUNCH!

WE'VE GOT TO PROVE OUR SUPERIORITY OVER WOMEN!

LET'S SCRATCH THEM WITH OUR BEARDS!

HOW CAN WE GAIN SUPREMACY OVER WOMEN ?

WE'LL STAVE IN THEIR SKULLS!

NO, STUPID! WE'VE GOT TO BE SUBTLE!

WE'LL THREATEN TO STAVE IN THEIR SKULLS!

WHO'S THAT?
IT LOOKS SOMETHING LIKE THOR.

HERE IS MY NEW VARIATION OF THE WHEEL --I CALL IT THE HOOP.

BUT WHAT HAPPENED TO YOU ?
--YOU'RE SO CYLINDRICAL!

--IT EVENTUALLY HONES YOU DOWN!

THIS COULD CHANGE THE WHOLE COURSE OF HISTORY!

THERE'S NOTHING NASTIER THAN LIVING IN A DIRTY CAVE.

UNLESS IT'S BEING A BROOM.

TO GET ANYWHERE IN THIS WORLD YOU HAVE TO THINK BIG!
?
THAT'S THE MOST RIDICULOUS THING I'VE EVER HEARD OF!
?

I'VE INVENTED A MUSICAL INSTRUMENT.

TWANG

WHAT CAN ANYBODY PLAY WITH ONLY ONE STRING ?

ROCK AND ROLL?

THE BLACK NEANDERTHAL GOES ON THE RED CRO-MAGNON.

HOW SIMPLE IT ALL IS!

JUST SAIL OUT FAR ENOUGH -

FALL OFF THE EDGE -

AND YOU'RE IN OUTER SPACE.